For my children,
Olivia, Cassandra and Alexander,
who teach me that life truly is magic...

And to all the adults reading this book.
I don't care who you are. If a child
wants to show you something
they are proud of, you act impressed.

abra-KID-abra
Copyright © 2015 by Christopher James
funnyhypermagic.com

Printed in the United States of America
ISBN: 978-0-9855789-5-4

Hello my new magical friend.

For as long as I can remember, magic has been
a part of my life. Now, as my family's gift to you,
we are proud to share some of our secrets. Magic is
a great way to make new friends and can change your
entire life. From this day on, you will never be the same.

As a student, I was very shy and quiet. Once, I found my first
magic book, that all changed. My life was never the same. I hope, in
some small way, I can influence you to expand your thinking, use your
imagination, and unleash the magic that lies within you!

RUBBER PENCIL

Effect: The magician's solid wand or pencil seems to turn to soft rubber. On command, it turns solid again.

Secret: Hold the wand horizontally in front of you between thumb and forefinger about a third of the way from the end. By moving your hand up and down in short quick moves, the wand will seem to become flexible and appear as if it were made of rubber (see illustration). This is an excellent optical illusion.

Presentation: Tap the wand on something to show that it is solid. Say the magic word and now demonstrate that it is wobbly and flexible. Another magic word and it turns solid again.

QUARTER BACK

Ask your kid brother if he'd like to earn a quarter. Tell him that if he can tear a piece of paper into 4 equal parts, you'll give him a quarter!
He will carefully do so... then demand his quarter! (now, this part is fun!)
You hand him one of the 4 pieces of paper, and say, "Here is your quarter."
(of the paper)

A QUARTER

What did one eye say to the other?
Between you and I, something smells!

What do you get if you cross a duck and a firework?
A firequaker!

Why don't actrobats work in the winter?
They only do Summer-saults

What happened when the lion ate the comedian?
He felt funny!

What do you give a sick bird?
Tweetment!

LAST STRAW

FIG. 1

Thread a length of string through a paper straw. Bend the straw then cut the straw (fig. 1). The string will remain unhurt!
Follow the directions shown below and you can do this trick!

Secretly cut silt on one side of the straw, in the middle. When you bend the straw, the thread will fall through the slit away from the middle of the straw. When you cut the middle of the straw, the scissors will go above the string. To finish, pull out the string unharmed, and crumple the straw in the other hand.

STRING

JUMPING BAND

Put a rubber band around your first and second fingers so that it looks like figure 1 from the front. As you stretch the rubber band, secretly pull all your fingertips inside the band. This is not seen by the audience.

Tell them the rubber band will amazingly jump across to the other two fingers. All you need to do is straighten out your fingers, and the band will move to the other fingers as in figure 3.

**DO NOT EVER
SHOW THIS SIDE
OF YOUR HAND**

1.

2.

3.

ELBOW GREASE

Show everyone a single coin. Tell all that by rubbing your elbow with it, you can change it into two coins! And you do it!

Before doing this trick hide a similar coin in your collar (Fig. 1) as you rub your elbow, grasp the hidden coin and, as you bring your hands together, you can show your audience two coins where there was once just one!!!

FIG. 1

HIDDEN COIN

RUB COIN
ON
ELBOW

ACROBATIC CLIPS

Fold a dollar bill in a "S" shape, and attach two paperclips as shown below. Tell everybody that the paperclips will be launched into the air, and in the middle of their acrobatic flight, will come together and impossibly link...right in mid-air!

With a drumroll, pull the two ends of the bill sharply in opposite directions. The clips will come together and jump into the air all by themselves. Now you just need to catch the paperclips, show them linked together, and take your bow!

MAGICAL
APPEARING WORDS

```
D E W W G W X O D H S A
T A H P O T S G O F E M
V K I N C A E U O Y S A
S P L E R W D B N L Z Z
O K H Z W I A E O N E I
N U C R N A P I I U R N
I H Z I O Q S V C B G G
O D F B R U F W X B U J
B T Q R L T O Z P I Z J
Y D D L B W E K F U X Z
R F I M B J C R M V R A
M A G I C I A N D C L G
```

AMAZING
BUNNY
HOUDINI
ILLUSIONS
MAGICIAN
TOP HAT
ACE OF
SPADES
TRICKS
WOW

FUNNY STUFF

What do Porcupines say to each other when they shake hands?

"Ouch!"

How do you know that carrots are good for your eyesight?

Have you ever seen a rabbit wearing glasses?

What kind of cat shouldn't you play cards with?

A Cheetah!

How do you make an elephant float?

Add an elephant to 2 scoops of vanilla ice cream & some milk!

What has no beginning, no end, and nothing in the middle?

A doughnut!

COLOR SENSE

What the Audience sees: You amazingly identify the color of a crayon handed to you behind your back only by touching it.

Super-Secret Tricky Method: Ask someone to take any crayon from a box and hand it to you behind your back. Make sure you don't see it!
You then turn to face the audience but keep the crayon behind your back. Secretly dig your right thumb-nail into the crayon wax. Keep hold of the crayon behind your back as you bring your right hand up to your forehead as if concentrating. Take a quick peek at your thumbnail and you will see bits of crayon in it and will know the chosen color.
Fake concentrating some more and then dramatically announce the color!

MARK
THUMBNAIL
WITH CRAYON

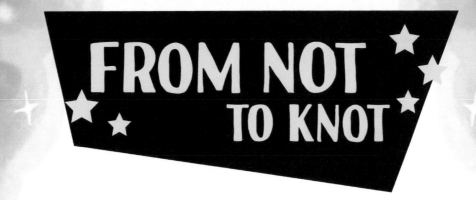

FROM NOT TO KNOT

Effect: A knot mysteriously appears in the corner of a handkerchief.

Secret: Before your performance, secretly tie a knot in one corner of a handkerchief. Show the handkerchief but hold it with the knot hidden in your right hand.

The left hand now lifts the bottom end of the handkerchief and places it in the right hand along with the top corner. Give the handkerchief a shake and drop the unknotted end.

Repeat this three times. On the third attempt allow the knotted corner to drop, retaining your grip on the other corner. All you have done is change the corner you are holding but it appears that the knot has formed by magic.

KNOT

THIRD TIME
DROP
KNOTTED END

PENCIL POWER

Effect: The magician makes some mysterious passes around a wand or pencil which uncannily starts to move on its own.

Secret: The magician secretly blows on the wand, which causes it to roll.

Props: Use a wand or pencil, and a smooth table-top.

Preparation: Practice blowing toward the wand gently and secretly.

Presentation: Lay the wand on the table and very slowly trace circles around the outside of the wand with a finger. Then, as you move the finger away, the wand seems to follow. You claim to have created static field that pulls plastic like a magnet. The trick is that as you draw the finger away from you and from the wand, you blow gently on the wand. The audience is so busy watching the movement of the finger, they won't notice that you are blowing towards the wand, which causes it to roll easily on th flat surface.

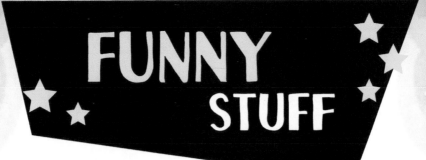

Why did the cow cross the road?
To get to the udder side!

What did the grape do when it got stepped on?
It let out a little wine!

What dog keeps the best time?
A watch dog!

How do you make a tissue dance?
Put a little boogey in it!

What did the water say to the boat?
Nothing, it just waved!

VANISHING ★RUBBER BANDS

Wrap a rubber band around the tips of both your middle fingers (fig. 1). On the edge of a table, show these two fingers (fig. 2).

FIG. 1

FIG. 2

Place both hands under the table edge (fig. 3). Then show both index fingers and say, "The rubber bands have disappeared!) (fig. 4).
Place both hands under the table again, then show both middle fingers. With a surprised look on you face declare, "The rubber bands have reappeared!".

FIG. 3

FIG. 4

X-RAY VISION

Ask someone to thoroughly shuffle a deck of cards. The cards are handed to you and you put them into the box they came in. You now remove the cards, one by one, but name each card before removing them!
You have, beforehand cut out a little window in the box. This allows you to see the name of the card you are about to show!

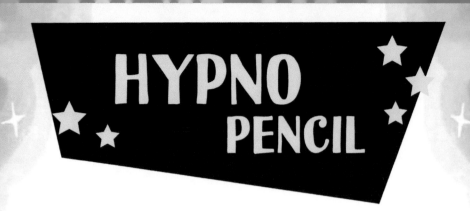

HYPNO
PENCIL

Tell your friends that you can hypnotize an ordinary lead pencil and make it write any color they ask you to!
"Make it write red!" says one. So with a flourish, do just that!
Any other color is just as easy to do!

RING THING

Tell your pals that you can do an impossible trick!

You say that you can push your whole hand through a finger ring you are holding in your hand!

Of course none of them will believe you! With a big smile, put your finger through the ring and poke your hand.
You are "pushing" your hand through the ring!

MULTIPLYING COINS

You place 4 coins on the table. You now tell your friends that you can, with your mysterious powers, cause the 4 coins to convert into 5.

Secretly, you have attached a coin (with a dab of soap) to the underside of the table, brush the coins into your cupped left hand and at the same time release the hidden coin. Immediately make a fist around the coins, ask someone to touch your fist, then open your hand, and behold...there are five coins!

RELEASE HIDDEN COIN

FUNNY STUFF

Why don't skeletons fight each other?
The don't have the guts!

What do you get if you cross a sheepdog with a rose?
A collie-flower!

Why did the pony cough?
Because he was a little horse!

What gets wetter the more it dries?
A towel!

What goes up and down but does not move?
A staircase!

DO MAGIC
★ WITH A PENCIL

Print the word **FUN** as shown here.

Now follow the example below to finish the drawing.
"Who has more **FUN** than a clown" you say when you are finished!

FLOATING CUP

Preparation: Before the show, make a loop of clear tape and stick it to the back of the cup. This should form a little handle just big enough for your thumb to fit through.

Tip: Always have the audience sit directly in front of you so they don't have a side view of the props or your hands. This trick doesn't work if people can see the cup handle, so you'll need a bit of distance between you and your audience.

Hold the cup in both hands with your thumbs in the back. Slip one of your thumbs into the loop of tape. Tell the audience that now the cup will magically float in the air.

Slowly spread your fingers away from the cup. Now the cup appears to be floating!

PECULIAR PAPER TEAR

You show a 4"x 4" square of tissue paper.
Proceed to tear it into small pieces into a ball, squeezing it as you do so, with a shout of "presto", unroll the ball and the piece of paper is whole and restored!
Before presenting this trick, roll a duplicate 4"x 4" tissue into a ball, and hide it in your hand. When doing this stunt, simply trade places with the torn pieces and the whole pieces, while you are going thru the squeezing motion.

WHOLE PIECE HIDDEN
DO NOT SHOW

WHOLE PIECE

TEAR THIS   TORN PIECES

TRADE
PIECES

MAGIC WITH A HAT

Place a hat on a drinking glass.
Now, drop a few coins into the hat and look and behold! One of the coins falls right through the hat into the drinking glass!

Secret: To do this amazing trick, secretly place a coin on the glass rim. The weight of the hat will hold it in place. As you drop the coins into the hat, slightly lift the brim of the hat and the coin will fall into the glass.

HIDDEN COIN

BAFFLING BANDS

Effect: Three loops of paper are cut with surprising results.

Secret: You need three strips of paper, each about five centimetres by one metre. Glue the ends of the first strip together to form a loop. Do the same with the secon strip but give one end a half turn before gluing the ends. In making the third loop give the paper one complete turn before gluing. Cut down the centre of the first loop with a pair of scissors. This will make two loops as one would expect.
When the second loop is cut in the same way it forms one extra large loop and the third one produces thow loops linked together.

EQUALS   EQUALS   EQUALS

COOL TRICK

What you need: Plastic cup that you cannot see through, sponge cut to fit very tightly into the bottom of the cup, ice cube, pitcher with less than 1/4 inch of cold water in it.

Preparation: Before the show, push the sponge down into the bottom of the cup so that it's very snug and won't fall out. Put the ice cube on the sponge. Tell the audience that your breath comes from the North Pole and can freeze water.

Pour the water into the cup. Blow into the cup as the sponge fills with water, all the water should be absorbed into the sponge. Turn the cup over. The ice cube will fall out! Now say, "Wonder if my breath would help stop global warming!"

SPONGE

ICE CUBE

SPONGE

SELF-SLICING BANANA

What you need: Banana, strong sewing needle, paper towels.

Preparation: Before the show, get the banana ready. Push the needle carefully into the top third of the banana until it hits the skin on the other side. Move the needle from side to side to cut through the banana, but don't make a big hole. Do the same thing in the bottom third of the banana. This may get messy, so keep a paper towel nearby to wipe the needle and your hands. Rub the holes gently to close them.

Onstage, tell the audience that you can communicate with bananas. Hold the banana up so they can see that it is not peeled.

Put the banana down on a paper towel. Speak to the banana and tell it that you need three pieces to share with friends.

Unpeel the banana and ta-da! The banana seems to have sliced itself!

DISAPPEARING PAPER CLIP

What you need: Paper clip, small but fairly strong magnet, long-sleeved shirt with cuffs that fit snugly to wear at the show.

Preparation: Before you go onstage, prepare your shirt. Hide the magnet in the cuff of one of your sleeves. Make sure you have the active side of the magnet facing down. Your cuff should be tight enough to hold the magner in place. If not, tape it to the inside of your cuff.

Say you'll make the paper clip disappear just by waving your hands over it. Wave both hands over the clip, making them cross each other while saying "Paper clip, get thee gone! Disappear and vanish!". Keep the sleeve with the magnet in it on the bottom.
Move your hands right above the clip so that they're almost touching it. The paper clip should cling to the bottom of your sleve. Slowly uncross your hands, and announce in a dramatic voice that the paper clip has vanished!

TRANSFER STRENGTH

Call for a volunteer to come onstage, and ask him to try to lift you off the ground. After the volunteer puts you back down, announce that if you touch a special spot under his chin it'll impossible for him to pick you up again. Claim that by touching the spot, you'll be able to steal all his strength and transfer it to yourself. Touch several places under the volunteer's chin as if you are trying to decide where the special spot it. Frown a little bit as you do this, and then smile when you "find" it.

Ask the volunteer to grab both your upper arms. Then tell him to try to lift you. Keep your finger underneath his chin, and as he stats to pick you up, carefully and gently push his head up and back with your finger, saying "Give me your strength!". Keep gently pushing, and if you get your timing right, it'll be impossible for him to lift you!

TRACKING THE FACTS

When you gently push someone's chin up and back, it puts him off balance, and he can't lift you.

What starts with a P and ends with an E and has a million letters in it?
Post Office!

What gets bigger and bigger the more you take away?
Holes!

What breaks when you say it?
Silence!

Why did the teacher wear sunglasses?
Because his class was so bright!

What do you call cheese that isn't yours?
Nacho cheese!

THE BENT SPOON

Grip the spoon as shown, hold at angle indicated, and with apparent effort, appear to bend the spoon almost in half.
Then snap your fingers over the spoon and show that it is restored.

FIG. 1

FIG. 2

FIG. 3

FIG. 4

THROUGH A POSTCARD

Effect: A postcard is cut so it will go over your body.

Secret: Boast that you can walk through a postcard then make the following moves. Fold the postcard in half lengthways.
Make as many cuts as possible from the edge of the card to the centre and from the centre towards the edges as shown.
The more cuts you make the easier the trick is to do. Unfold the card and cut along the centre, from A to B. You can now open out the card into a large loop that will easily go over your body.

CARD FOLDED

REMOVE YOUR THUMB

Follow the directions shown in figures 1, 2 and 3.

FIG. 1

FIG. 2

FIG. 3

This takes a little practice.
Now you can have fun removing your thumb before your squeemish friends.

FRONT VIEW

MAGIC HOLE
IN HAND

Make a tube from a piece of paper. Hold it up to your eye to look through it. Along side of the tube hold your hand open as shown in the drawing. Be sure to keep both eyes wide open and you will see a hole in your hand!

**Stay in touch with
Christopher James**

**Facebook:
www.facebook.com/funnyhypermagic**

**Website:
funnyhypermagic.com**

**Twitter:
@funnyhypermagic**

**Email
abrakidabra@funnyhypermagic.com**

23391743R00024

Made in the USA
Columbia, SC
14 August 2018